Thank You
FOR LEADING

A Gift for Managers

TO:

_____

_____

_____

FROM:

_____

_____

_____

NOTE:

_____

_____

_____

_____

_____

_____

_____

_____

_____

_____

_____

_____

Thank You

FOR LEADING

A Gift for Managers

RALPH PETERSON

Thank You for Leading: *A Gift for Managers*

Copyright © 2025 by Ralph Peterson.

Published by Four-Nineteen Press

For inquiries visit: www.ralphpeterson.com

ISBN: 979-8-9919583-2-5

Printed in the United States of America

This book is dedicated to everyone whoever said Yes, to leadership.

Thank You.

Chapter One

The letter sat on my desk, unopened all morning. I found it in my mailbox when I came in. It was an internal letter. No name or return address on it. No stamp; just my name written neatly across the sealed envelope; MR. PETERSON. It was written in big block letters indicating its author was male. Likely a disgruntled resident or maybe an employee, though I doubted an employee would've taken the time or effort to write a letter. I felt the weight of it, heavy, at least a couple pages, and tried to imagine who could've written it but I had no idea. I took in some air and set it off to the side of my desk for later.

There's an old management adage that says, "If you find yourself eating a crap filled sandwich, you probably ordered it." I looked at the envelope and felt certain it contained a crap filled sandwich and worse, I was sure I ordered it. *Only four weeks into the job and I'm already getting handwritten letters,* I thought. Not good.

The phone on my desk rang, taking my attention away from the envelope and my day officially began. I had a call out on the second floor, and the third-floor house-keeper was running late, as usual. As I stepped out of my office to find a coffee, one of the floor techs walked up and told me he talked to his Union Representative and was told he didn't have to fill in for housekeeping if he didn't want to. He was tall and lanky, close to my age, if not older. I paused, mid step and almost started to argue with him when I noticed his uniform. Clean and tucked in for once. I smiled. Progress. I patted him on the shoulder and assured him I had no intention of asking him to change jobs today.

"But good morning," I said and kept walking. He didn't respond and I didn't look back. I headed toward the kitchen, pulling a used hairnet out of my pocket as I walked in. Donna, the food service manager greeted me with a half-smile and quickly looked around the kitchen to make sure everyone else was wearing a hairnet. I didn't. I walked straight to the coffee machine, grabbed a red plastic cup and poured some. I leaned back against the tray line and took a sip. "Ah!" I said, enjoying my first cup of the day. A young, heavy-set girl who was busy setting up the tray line, laughed at me.

"You're the only person I know who likes our coffee," she said. I reached over and added more to my cup.

"It's the only coffee I drink," I said. She laughed.

"Seriously? You don't make coffee at home?" I shook my head.

"Nope. I don't even own a coffee maker."

"Seriously!?" she said. She couldn't believe it. I had everyone's attention now. I laughed.

"True story," I said. "Why buy coffee when I can get it here for free." I looked around for some playful banter, but everyone just kind of looked at me funny. I shrugged, finished the coffee, rinsed the cup in the sink and set it off to the side.

"It smells great in here, by the way," I said to Donna on my way out. She perked up a bit and smiled but didn't say anything.

The nursing home was shaped like the letter U, with two 40 bed long term care units on the 2nd and 3rd floors and one 20 bed short term care unit on the 1st floor. It's located in a busy suburb of Buffalo New

York and still is, by far, one of the worst nursing homes I had ever managed. Not only was it dirty, from top to bottom, and everything was broken or chipped, and haphazardly duct taped together, (the furniture, the medical equipment, heck, even the window blinds), but the staff were just as rough.

Years of neglect, low wages and ongoing union battles had hardened them against management to the point where every conversation teetered on the edge of a full-blown argument. I had learned quickly to fight fire with fire. I talked fast and I walked fast. I never gave anyone time to argue or pushback. Talk and move... talk and move... that was my strategy.

I took the stairs, two at a time, to the third floor and began to make rounds. I stopped in each resident's room to say hello and make a list of everything that needed to get done. There were so many issues and projects, that I found myself having to rec-reate my list of priorities every single day.

It was just after 10am by the time I made my way down to the 2nd floor. I'd forgot-ten the 2nd floor housekeeper had called out and it took me a minute to get my head around how dirty it was. Used gloves, paper towels and soiled linen littered the hall-ways. It didn't smell bad, so that was good, but it sure did look terrible.

I walked over to the housekeeping closet,

pulled out the cart and began to put on a pair of gloves.

"Did you get my letter?"

I spun around to see Mr. Addison, one of the residents sitting in a wheelchair and smiling at me. It took me a second to recognize him.

"You're the one who wrote me the letter?" I said. He looked confused.

"Who else?" he said. I shrugged and laughed. I should have known. Mr. Addison had led a resident uprising against me the first week I was here.

"No. I didn't get a chance to look at it yet. I'm sorry." I pushed the housekeeping cart back into the closet, closed the door and faced him. "What did it say?" I said bracing myself for the avalanche of complaints. He stared back at me, slack jawed.

"Just read the letter," he said impatiently and wheeled himself away.

I stood there for a minute, watching him go and realized I had never seen him out of bed before. I walked to the nurse's station and asked one of the nurses.

"Is it my imagination or is this the first time he's been out of bed in weeks?" The nurse looked where I was looking and nodded.

"He's been getting up more and more over the last couple of day's", she said. "He's making good progress."

I stood there for a few more minutes and watched him roll down the hall and turn into his room. I thought about putting it off. About going back to the housekeeping closet and making my rounds and cleaning the rooms before heading back downstairs and reading the letter, but there was something about his demeanor.

"Did you get my letter?" His tone wasn't accusatory, it was happy. In fact, it seemed like he thought I was going to be happy.

"I'll be back," I said to the nurse and headed for the stairs.

The letter was where I left it. I sat down, took a deep breath and opened the envelope.

Mr. Peterson,

I hope this letter finds you well. I've been meaning to write to you for some time now. As a new resident here, I've seen my fair share of ups and downs, but I felt compelled to express my thoughts on the recent changes I've witnessed.

When you first arrived, I'll admit I was skeptical. Your direct approach and no-nonsense attitude rubbed me the wrong way. I even found myself joining in with others, grumbling about how you handled things. But something shifted over the past few weeks.

I've watched as the halls became cleaner, staff more attentive, and the overall atmosphere transformed. Your straightforwardness, which I once took for rudeness, I've come to understand as dedication. You've accomplished what many couldn't, and it's inspired me to reflect on my own behavior.

I want to apologize for my initial resistance and thank you for not giving up on us. Your commitment to improving our living conditions has not gone unnoticed, and I respect the strength it must take to make these changes.

Thank you for being the leader we needed, even when we didn't realize it. Your perseverance has brought hope to an old man like me, and for that, I am truly grateful.

Sincerely,

Rich Addison

I shifted in my chair, took another deep breath and reread the letter, slower this time. Then I read it again. Despite my best efforts, my eyes watered each time. I read it again.

I've spent many years in various levels of leadership and have come to understand being called a manager, supervisor, or a leader in any capacity are fancy titles that are designed to sugarcoat the truth. The truth is, I'm not really in charge of anyone; rather I'm responsible for everyone. That is what I would have told you, if you asked me before Mr. Addison wrote me this letter. I would have defined leadership as a burden of responsibility and not much more. However, after reading and rereading Mr. Addison's letter, I now see it differently. Leadership isn't just a burden; it's also a gift. A gift we give to our customers, our staff and our organizations.

I slid the letter back in the envelope and once again, set it off to the side. I wiped my face with my hands and my hands on my pants and went back up the stairs.

"B-51!" I heard Kimberly, the activities director, call out as I stepped out of the stairwell. "B-51!" Bingo, the number one game in every nursing home I've ever been in, was in full swing. I waved to Kimberly, not expecting to see Mr. Addison, but there he was, sitting at the table, fully engaged. He had his back to me. Kimberly nodded and smiled in my direction and Mr. Addison saw it and spun around. We looked at each other for a full minute as Kimberly spun the cage of numbered balls waiting for another number to appear. Mr. Addison smiled thoughtfully and put his thumb up. I nodded and returned the gesture.

"Thank you," I mouthed. His smile widened and he nodded. I pulled a new pair of disposable gloves from my pocket and returned to the housekeeping closet.

Chapter Two

It was nearly 5pm, when I finally got into my car and headed home. In the early hours of the morning the drive to work takes less than 30 minutes. At this time of the day, however, it takes twice as long. I don't mind it though. Usually, I would just pass the time listening to a podcast or singing along to old time country music, unwinding from a long day. But not today. Today I sat in traffic silently staring off into space. An impatient horn blared behind me, pulling me back to reality. I waved apologetically.

I left Mr. Addison's letter, sitting on the edge of my desk at work, but it was the only thing I thought about. "Thank you," he wrote. "For being the leader, we needed..." I smiled in spite of myself as I followed the flow of traffic from Eastern Avenue to Park, and then made my way onto 95, heading West. I pulled in behind a big eighteen-wheeler and stared at his taillights.

Years ago, long before I became a management consultant, traveling from one organization to another, writing books and giving lectures about my experiences, my dad gave me a piece of advice that I never quite understood, or really believed—until now.

It was early in my career, and I was

struggling to lead a difficult team when my dad and I met for lunch. He asked me how it was going. It was one of those times when, at first, you're eager to share all the wins, all the great moments but then, just before you open your mouth, you're quickly reminded of all the losses. It's like finding yourself in a small boat being tossed around in a large ocean, one minute you're up and then the next minute you're down, a victim to the ebb and flow of leadership. I eventually just shrugged and smiled, not sure what to say.

"That's the thing about being in charge," he said, as if he could hear my inner dialogue. "We never focus on the good stuff." I shifted in my seat and picked up the menu. My dad, like all dads, had an uncanny knack for spinning everything positively. A skinned knee? Nope. A scar worth bragging about. Lost the race? Nope. We'll get them next time. Girl problems? Nope. Maybe she isn't the right one.

"It's important for you to know this," he said, putting down his coffee and hesitating long enough for me to look up and meet him eye to eye. "People need you; they respect you; they are happy you are there, leading from the front. Not a lot of people are willing to do it." He leaned forward a bit, never taking his eyes off me. "The problem is, you have to know it and believe it, deep down, because no one will ever tell you." I nodded, tight-lipped, and smiled.

I still didn't know what to say, so I looked back at the menu.

Here's a fun fact. Did you know, statistically speaking, you are three times more likely to receive a greeting card–acknowledging a failed relationship or a divorce, than you are to receive a Happy Boss's Day greeting card. Can you believe that? Hallmark sells more "Congratulations On Your Divorce–Time To Party," cards, than they sell "Thank You For Leading," cards.

To say management is a thankless job, is an understatement. Perhaps the understatement of all understatements.

But here's the thing, like my dad said, and Mr. Addison confirmed, agreeing to take on a leadership role, in any capacity is a gift. It is one of the most selfless acts a non-family member can give another person. If someone says, "I will be responsible for you. I will look out for you. You can trust me." Then the only reasonable thing to say to someone who does that for you is, thank you. But don't hold your breath.

I've been managing ever since I was sixteen years old. I've held dozens of leadership positions, in just as many organizations, both as a paid employee and as a management consultant, for 31 years before I ever received a single thank you letter. And when I did (finally) get a Thank You letter, it was from a customer (Mr. Addison), not an employee.

This, in part, is the reason I wanted to

write this book. I know how rare and how impactful a simple gesture, like saying thank you, can have on a manager. Honestly, I'd be lying if I told you that I didn't know where I put Mr. Addison's letter–the one I received nearly a decade ago. I know exactly where it is, and I reread it often.

The second reason I wrote this book* is because I know how challenging it is to be an effective manager. I have been promoted and demoted, hired and fired from all kinds of management positions. And in the pages that follow, I am going to share with you everything I've learned, the good, the bad and the ugly. I'm not going to hold

---

* This mini book, Thank You for Leading: A Gift for Managers, are the first two chapters of a larger book of the same title: Thank You For Leading by Ralph Peterson.

anything back. But first, let me say what everyone else should have already said:

Thank you.

Thank you for coming in
early and staying late.

Thank you for coming in on Saturdays and Sundays, even when you didn't have to.

Thank you for working on your birthday.

Thank you for braving the snowstorms.

Thank you for spending
your holidays with us.

Thank you for making sure
the jobs got done.

A Gift for Managers

Thank you for doing the jobs that didn't.

Thank you for spending your own
money to buy your team coffee,
donuts, pizza, and soft drinks.

Thank you for training and retraining
your staff. And thank you for
training them again. And again.

Thank you for covering.

Thank you for speaking up
for your customers.

Thank you for speaking up for your staff.

Thank you for speaking up
for your company.

Thank You FOR LEADING

Thank you for always coming to
the rescue, no matter the cost.

Thank you for putting up a fight.

Thank you for listening
with an open heart.

Thank you for sharing your time.

Thank you for sharing your shoulder.

Thank you for giving people
second chances.

Thank you for giving credit
when it is deserved.

A Gift for Managers

Thank you for stepping back from the spotlight, even when you've earned it.

Thank you for saying yes when you can and no when you have to.

Thank you for dealing with the eye rolls, the back talk, and the attitudes.

Thank you for leading by example.

Thank you for being brave.

Thank you for being strong.

Thank you for being dependable.

Thank you for being stable.

Thank You FOR LEADING

Thank you for being responsible.

Thank you for not quitting.

Thank you for having conviction.

Thank you for standing up
for what is right.

Thank you for not showing
your frustration.

Thank you for your skepticism.

Thank you for your wisdom.

Thank you for your attention.

Thank you for your patience.

A Gift for Managers

Thank you for your love.

Thank you for your dedication.

Thank you for your understanding.

Thank you for not using the
word 'burnout' as an excuse.

Thank you for looking past the pettiness
and focusing on the solutions.

Thank you for reading.

Thank you for debating.

Thank you for being a good investigator.

Thank you for not taking my word for it.

Thank You FOR LEADING

Thank you for not taking their word for it.

Thank you for being the
bearer of bad news.

Thank you for always being there.

Thank you for taking your employees' side.

Thank you for taking your customers' side.

Thank you for taking the
organization's side.

Thank you for always being dependable.

Thank you for the late nights
and the early mornings.

A Gift for Managers

Thank you. For all of it. For everything. Thank You for Leading.

RALPH PETERSON is a Management Development Coach, Keynote Speaker, and Best Selling Author with over three decades of experience helping managers lead with clarity and confidence. As the founder of Ralph Peterson Management Services, Ralph combines grit, humor, and real-world insight to support leaders through every stage of their journey.

Interested in bringing Ralph
to your organization?

VISIT: *www.ralphpeterson.com*

EMAIL: *ralph@ralphpeterson.com*

www.ingramcontent.com/pod-product-compliance
Lightning Source LLC
Chambersburg PA
CBHW020813130626
46554CB00006B/2412